CONTENTS

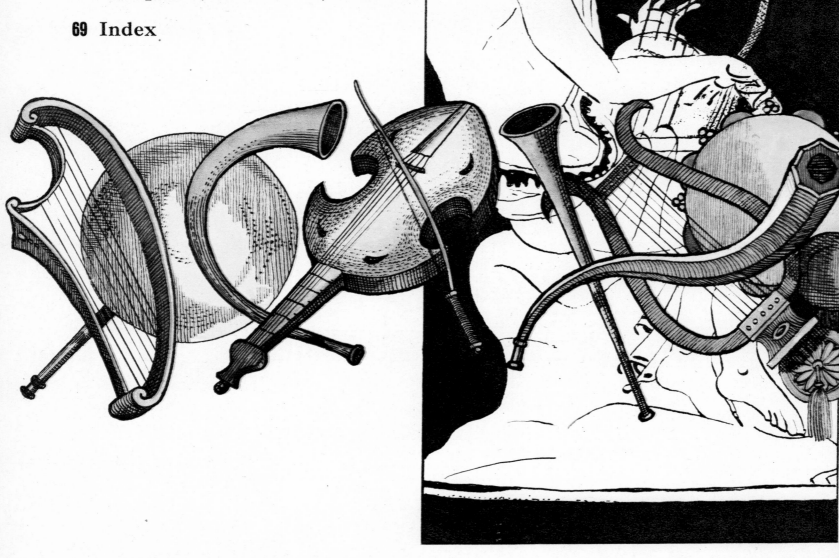

Produced by Rathbone Books, London.　•　Printed in Great Britain by L.T.A. Robinson Limited, London

the Story of Music

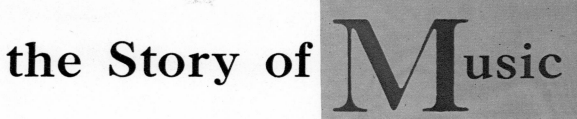

Benjamin Britten
Imogen Holst

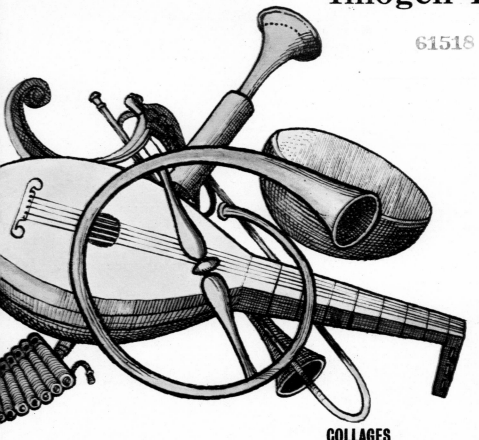

COLLAGES
Ceri Richards

© 1958, Benjamin Britten, Imogen Holst and Adprint Limited **RATHBONE BOOKS LONDON**

Sound and Rhythm

No one knows how long ago the first music was made. The Stone Age men who painted pictures on the walls of caves in France and Spain thousands of years before anybody had invented writing, may have sung songs or played tunes on a bone whistle, perhaps to frighten away the evil spirits at the end of a day's hunting. But we shall never know what they sang or played, for tunes cannot be dug up. We can guess that prehistoric men danced and sang, because music flourishes among those who are still living a primitive life.

Sound and rhythm existed on the earth's surface millions of years before there were any men to hear them. The waves of the sea are never still: their sounds change from high to low, and their rhythms change from quick to slow.

Many composers have been interested in these sounds, and have tried to write sea-music. What they have written has seldom been an attempt to reproduce the *exact* sound of the wind and the waves: a cymbal crash can never sound just like a splash; but it can suggest one. A work of art is not a slavish copy of nature; it is artificial in the original sense of the word, which means 'made with skill'. Whether he is a composer or a painter, an artist needs to have courage and imagination as well as energy and skill, for he has to create something that will not only have a life of its own, with the vitality of nature, but will also last for centuries.

A painted wave can give us such a vivid impression of the sea that we can almost feel the weight of the water and the sting of the spray. A real wave breaks and disperses; the painted wave remains poised, and yet exciting, for as long as there are people to look at it. The sound of a real wave breaking may never happen again in just that particular way, but the sounds a composer creates when he writes a musical conversation between wind and waves can be repeated whenever there is an orchestra to play and an audience to listen.

The composer writes in the language of music, which can be as clear and concise as the language of words. Musicians who are thoroughly at home in their own language can read the printed symbols of sea-music on this page as easily as they can read printed words. There is no need for them to take the book to a piano and 'try it over'; they can sit back and hear in their mind's ear the sounds as they rise and fall. To those who cannot read the written language of music this may seem like magic. It is a matter of learning and practice; no more miraculous than being able to read Greek poetry, or to follow the symbols of algebra in an equation, or to understand the words in this sentence.

A painter paints on canvas with brushes and tubes of coloured pigments, and with these simple, physical resources he creates art. In the same way, the resources of a composer are simple and physical; and all the sounds of a piece of music, high or low, loud or soft, long or short, quick or slow, can be written down on paper.

Courtesy Durand & Cie., Paris
In Debussy's 'La Mer' we feel the sea's atmosphere; in Hokusai's 'Great Wave' we sense its weight. Yet art does not copy nature.

Victoria and Albert Museum, London (Michael Holford)

Ripples spread across a pool much as sound-waves pass through the atmosphere: both travel outwards from a central area of disturbance.
John Gay

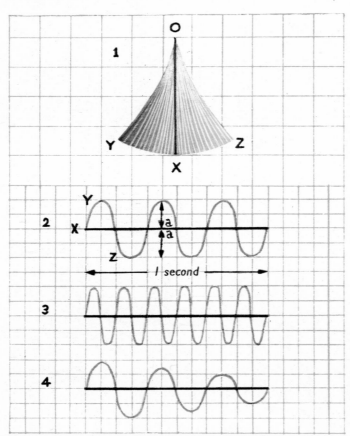

(1) X vibrates between Y and Z. (2) a is the amplitude of a vibration. (3) Six vibrations per second have a frequency twice as high as three. (4) Though amplitude fades, frequency is unchanged.

A sudden sound in the middle of a silence is like a pebble dropped into a pool: ripples travel outwards from the centre of disturbance. These ripples, or sound-waves, reach the ear and, through it, the brain.

Strike a bell and touch it; its surface quivers with vibrations. It is even possible to see these vibrations, though their to-and-fro movements are so rapid that the bell may just look blurred. The distance to-and-fro that a vibrating surface moves from its position of rest is the amplitude of the vibration. The greater the amount of energy used to produce a vibration, the greater its amplitude will be. The greater the amplitude, the louder the sound will be.

Loudness can be scientifically measured in units called decibels, of which 1 represents the softest sound that the human ear can detect. A single decibel only just crosses the threshold of hearing; a whisper measures 10–20 decibels; noisy conversation is about 70; a pneumatic drill equals 110; and any sound above 130 decibels, such as that of a low-flying plane, approaches the 'threshold of pain'.

To make a sound that we can hear, vibrations must be rapid. A bee buzzes, but a butterfly is silent because the movement of its wings is too slow to be audible. Our ears can hear sounds from about

Dr. M. S. Wood

Spectrogram showing the song of a European chaffinch with its variety of clear levels of pitch

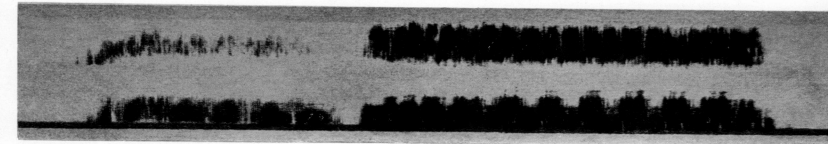

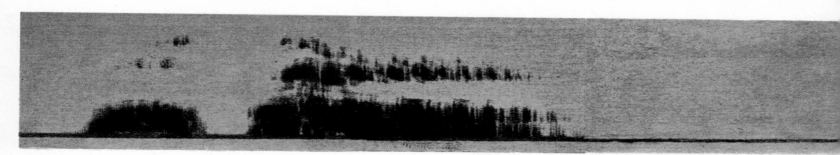

Spectrograms of a human voice singing and speaking the word 'Bra-vo'. In the sung word, the pitch remains steady; in the spoken, it falls.

Spectrograms by kind permission of Dr. W. H. Thorpe, F.R.S., and Miss Priscilla Pilcher

15 to 20,000 vibrations per second. In acoustics, which is the science of hearing, the number of vibrations per second is called frequency: the greater the frequency, the higher the sound.

The height or depth of a sound is called pitch. Only regular vibrations of unvarying frequency produce a definite level of pitch. In speech the pitch is always varying. Say the word 'no', trying to make it last for more than five seconds without letting your voice go up or down. If the sound remains level you will no longer be speaking; you will be singing.

When we listen to the birds singing we realise the innumerable possibilities of different levels of pitch. Birds are, in a sense, among the inventors of song, since they were singing millions of years before there were any men living on the earth.

When human beings sing, they prefer to limit themselves to a small number of definite, easily recognisable levels of pitch. These are called notes or tones. Many of the familiar tunes that are whistled or sung throughout Europe and America are founded on only seven notes. These are the notes that can be heard in a chime of bells, running up and down the steps of a ladder of sound: they can easily be picked out with one finger on the 'white notes' of a piano.

Long before there were any pianos, medieval European musicians sometimes found the pitch of their notes by taking goblets of the same size and pouring a different amount of water into each. It is an easy experiment to try: stand a row of glasses on a table and tap them with a spoon, one after another. The less water there is in a glass, the higher the note will be. You will find that the chiming ladder of notes, 1, 2, 3, 4, 5, 6, 7, will sound incomplete without its eighth step, called the octave. When the octave has been added, the row of glasses becomes a musical instrument. One can play tunes on it, finding the right notes by trial and error, while keeping the rhythm in mind.

Seven notes and the octave in a medieval chime of bells
British Museum

The leap of a ballet dancer takes time to complete. Only the stroboscopic photograph can capture its entire pattern in a single moment.
Gjon Mili

Music, like dancing, moves through time. We can never hear the whole shape of a tune at once, or see the whole pattern of a dance in a single moment. But when a tune or a dance is over, we find that we still hold in our minds some of the pattern which we have been following note by note or step by step.

Music sometimes flows freely, like conversation. More often its rhythm is measured, like metrical verse, with a recurring pulse going through it.

This pulse is not like the mechanical ticking of a clock, for rhythm in music is alive. It has physical tension and relaxation: a give-and-take as in the action of sawing a tree-trunk.

When a swimmer learns to swim he has to count to keep his movements rhythmical. All such actions become easier when they are done rhythmically. Rowers in a race keep time to the rhythm set by 'stroke'. Men hauling a rope avoid wasting energy by timing their efforts and pulling as one man.

In parts of Africa where farm work is not yet mechanised, field labourers often work in a rhythmical line, timing their steps so as to stamp the earth simultaneously. If they kept rigidly to a slow, monotonous 'STAMP . . . STAMP . . . STAMP . . .' the distance to be covered might seem endless. So they vary the rhythm, making a time-pattern with STEPS that are half as slow as a STAMP and with *hops* that are twice as quick as a STEP:

S T A M P	step·step	S T A M P	step·step
S T A M P	step·hop·hop	S T E P·hop·hop	S T E P·step

Millet painting from the Victoria and Albert Museum, London (Michael Holford)
In music, as in sawing a tree, there is a rhythmic give-and-take.

Or they may choose to divide its pulse into threes, and to use their STEP and hop to create an entirely different time-pattern, as in skipping:

STEP · hop	STEP · hop	hop · hop · hop	STEP · hop
hop · hop · hop	STEP · hop	STEP · hop	STEP · hop

Or they may vary the rhythm by combining twos and threes, keeping time with a pulse that is counted in fives, with a stress on one, two, *three*, four, five, or on one, two, three, *four*, five:

STEP · STEP · hop	hop · hop · STEP · hop	STEP · hop · STEP
hop · hop · hop · hop · hop	STEP · hop · STEP	hop · hop · STEP · hop

Or the combined twos and threes can be counted in sevens, with the stress either on *four* or *five*:

hop · STEP · hop · STEP · hop	hop · STEP · hop · hop · hop · hop
STEP · STEP · hop · hop · hop	STEP · STEP · hop · hop · hop

There are endless possibilities when one begins inventing time-patterns like these. However elaborate the rhythms may be, the units of time that make up each pattern can always be counted in twos or threes, or in multiples of two or three.

People who have studied African customs have described how road-makers and field workers will often take a drummer with them to help them by beating out a rhythm which keeps them going for hour after hour. When labourers work in this way there is little difference between the rhythm of their work and the rhythm of a dance.

Leonardo drawing reproduced by gracious permission of Her Majesty The Queen *British Museum (R. L. Jarmain)*

(Left) All physical actions are far easier when done rhythmically. **(Right)** Many African work-rhythms differ little from those of a dance.

Heraklion Museum, Crete
A Cretan 'Harvesters' Vase' of about 1500 B.C.

The earliest dances we know anything about were rituals to bring back the spring after winter, to make the crops grow and to celebrate the harvest. The picture of the ancient Cretan vase on this page shows a ritual procession of harvesters singing and dancing. We can tell by their attitudes – heads flung back and mouths wide open – that their dance was tremendously energetic and exciting.

Ritual of this kind is still an important part of civilised life in the Far East; on the Indonesian island of Bali events are still celebrated with an appropriate dance. Even in Europe we still find scattered survivals of ancient spring rituals.

In ritual dances rhythm is never casual: each step is important, for the dance may represent a matter of life and death. In our own music rhythm is equally important: as soon as it becomes casual, the sound is not worth listening to. An orchestral drummer, unlike a ritual dancer, reads his time-patterns from a printed page, but unless he plays with the purposeful vitality of a ritual dancer the music will not come to life.

Time-patterns are written with symbols which correspond with dancers' STAMP, STEP, hop. These symbols are referred to as 'notes', as they represent notes of different lengths. The method of writing

Captain Irving M. Johnson
A ceremonial dance on the Indonesian island, Bali, where ritual still plays a very important part in the lives of a highly civilised people.

Morris-dancing at Thaxted: revival of an ancient English custom
British Travel and Holidays Association

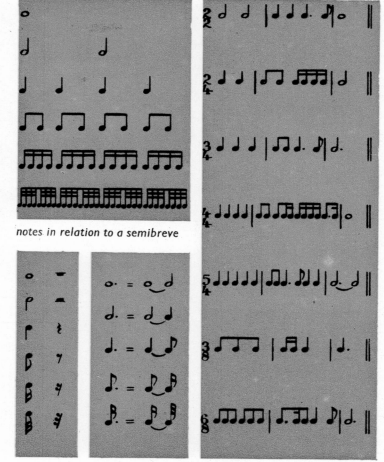

notes in relation to a semibreve

notes and rests – dotted notes – time-signatures and time-patterns

R. L. Jarmain
An orchestral drummer playing time-patterns from a printed page

them is described as 'notation'. The long STAMP of the primitive dancer is written ○ and is called a semibreve or whole note. The STEP which is half as long, is written ♩: a minim or half-note. The *hop* is written ♩: a crotchet or quarter-note. When a tail is added to a crotchet it becomes ♪: a quaver or eighth-note. A ♬ is a semiquaver, or sixteenth-note. A ♬ is a demisemiquaver or thirty-second-note. These last three notes are often grouped with their tails joined; there are examples on this page.

Every unit of time has a corresponding length of silence called a rest. A dot after any note or rest makes it half as long again. A curved line called a tie can be used to join two notes of equal pitch, making them sound like one continuous note.

The upright lines which mark the main pulse of the rhythm are called bar-lines. The distance between one bar-line and the next is called a bar or measure. At the beginning of the first bar of a piece of music, a symbol called a time-signature shows how its units are to be counted. This symbol is in the form of a fraction. The nominator (above) shows how many units the bar contains; and the denominator (below) shows the kind of units: 1 means a semibreve or whole-note ○; 2, a minim or half-note ♩; 4, a crotchet ♩; 8, a quaver ♪; and so on. Thus the 'fraction' ¾ means that each bar contains three crotchets or quarter-notes.

Written notes of any length can be placed high or low, in various definite positions, to represent all the different levels of pitch that may be needed in tunes which are to be played or sung.

Songs and Singers

The first European songs to be written down were Greek songs; and it is from the Greeks that we have learned to call notes of different pitch after the first seven letters of the alphabet – A, B, C, D, E, F and G. Greek scholars who studied music as a branch of mathematics measured the distance from one note to another between each of the eight rungs in a ladder of sound. The step between rungs B and C and between E and F is only half the size of the other steps: it is called a semitone. A to B, C to D, D to E, and F to G are whole tones. We can see and hear the difference on the piano: it has no 'black note' between B and C or E and F.

The ladder, or 'scale', of seven notes and the octave, which we have inherited from the Greeks, can begin on any note. The semitones (B to C and E to F) come on different steps or degrees of the scale, according to what the first note has been:

From A to A :	A $_{(1)}$ B $_{(\frac{1}{2})}$ C $_{(1)}$ D $_{(1)}$ E $_{(\frac{1}{2})}$ F $_{(1)}$ G $_{(1)}$ A
From B to B :	B $_{(\frac{1}{2})}$ C $_{(1)}$ D $_{(1)}$ E $_{(\frac{1}{2})}$ F $_{(1)}$ G $_{(1)}$ A $_{(1)}$ B
From C to C :	C $_{(1)}$ D $_{(1)}$ E $_{(\frac{1}{2})}$ F $_{(1)}$ G $_{(1)}$ A $_{(1)}$ B $_{(\frac{1}{2})}$ C
From D to D :	D $_{(1)}$ E $_{(\frac{1}{2})}$ F $_{(1)}$ G $_{(1)}$ A $_{(1)}$ B $_{(\frac{1}{2})}$ C $_{(1)}$ D
From E to E :	E $_{(\frac{1}{2})}$ F $_{(1)}$ G $_{(1)}$ A $_{(1)}$ B $_{(\frac{1}{2})}$ C $_{(1)}$ D $_{(1)}$ E
From F to F :	F $_{(1)}$ G $_{(1)}$ A $_{(1)}$ B $_{(\frac{1}{2})}$ C $_{(1)}$ D $_{(1)}$ E $_{(\frac{1}{2})}$ F
From G to G :	G $_{(1)}$ A $_{(1)}$ B $_{(\frac{1}{2})}$ C $_{(1)}$ D $_{(1)}$ E $_{(\frac{1}{2})}$ F $_{(1)}$ G

The position of the semitones is one of the most important things in all music; for tunes are founded on scales, and the shape and character of a tune depends to a large extent on where its semitones occur. Many of the tunes we sing today are founded on the C to C scale, with the semitones between the third and fourth, and between the seventh and eighth degrees. Other tunes, particularly some of the traditional folk-songs that go back for hundreds of years, are founded on the scales from A to A, or from D to D. The earliest Greek scale was from A to A; the four descending notes, A, G, F, E, were used as a basis for musical theory.

Greek musicians wrote their tunes by adding symbols above the words of the song, symbols for the notes C D E F G being written ꟼ ＜ Ⴖ Ｎ ⱬ. They wrote time-patterns above the notes in signs to indicate the number of time-units to each syllable: ‾ =2, ⌐ =3, ∪ =4, ⊔ =5.

Unfortunately few of these songs have survived. In spite of the great wealth of Greek lyric poetry and drama available to us today, less than a dozen Greek tunes remain. One of these, the Seikilos Song was borrowed by the early Christians, who altered the words, 'be happy always, as long as you live', to 'Hosanna to the Son of David'.

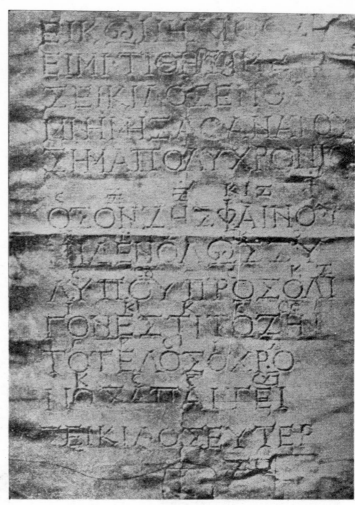

(Right) *Seikilos song c.100 B.C.: a rare example of ancient Greek music.* (Below) *Orpheus singing with his lyre: designed on a cup made c.440 B.C.*

Courtesy W. W. Norton & Co. Inc., Curt Sachs: 'The Rise of Music in the Ancient World'

State Museums, Berlin

16

King David the psalmist – from a medieval Jewish Bible
British Museum

וַיֹּאמֶר שְׁמוּאֵל אֶל שָׁאוּל אֹתִי שָׁלַח יְיָ לְמָשְׁחֲךָ לְמֶלֶךְ
עַל עַמּוֹ עַל יִשְׂרָאֵל וְעַתָּה שְׁמַע לְקוֹל דִּבְרֵי יְיָ
כֹּה אָמַר יְיָ צְבָאוֹת פָּקַדְתִּי אֵת אֲשֶׁר עָשָׂה עֲמָלֵק לְיִשְׂרָאֵל
אֲשֶׁר שָׂם לוֹ בַּדֶּרֶךְ בַּעֲלֹתוֹ מִמִּצְרָיִם עַתָּה לֵךְ וְהִכִּיתָ אֶת עֲמָלֵק

Jewish Bible manuscript. Accents show how words are to be chanted.
Courtesy Hebrew Union College Library, Cincinnati, Ohio

The earliest Christian church music was not only influenced by Greek song: it also followed the tradition of the music sung in the Jewish synagogues. This was a form of chanting, in which long sentences were sung on one note with occasional embellishments for the important words. Most of the texts for chanting were taken from the Book of Psalms, where the vivid language helped to transform spoken words into sung phrases.

Music needs words that are simple and direct. In the straightforward prose of the psalms all abstract ideas became real and familiar: one has only to open the book at random to come across a phrase such as, 'Set a watch, O Lord, before my mouth: keep the door of my lips.' In the psalms that were written by David himself there are dramatic changes of mood, from the despair of exile to the well-being and contentment of 'the pastures are clothed with flocks: the valleys also are covered over with corn.'

The verses of the psalms are nearly always divided into halves, each half expressing the same idea in a different way: 'O come, let us sing unto the Lord: let us make a joyful noise to the rock of our salvation.' In chanting a verse on one level of pitch, with the free rhythm of the spoken words, one's voice naturally tends to rise at the end of the first half and to fall at the end of the second half. This keeps the listeners' interest alive and helps to make the meaning clear.

It is more than likely that the early Christians sang in this sort of way, for we know from the

The early Christians of ancient Rome sought sanctuary underground, in narrow catacombs which echoed to their chanted hymns and psalms.

epistles of St. Paul that they had 'psalms and hymns and spiritual songs' whenever they met together. The Christians of Rome met secretly in the dark catacombs under the city, holding services by candlelight, and using the tombs of their saints for altars. The murmured chanting of psalms must have echoed mysteriously through the network of narrow passages. When Christianity became the established religion throughout the western Roman Empire and Byzantium, Christian communities were able to come above ground. They kept the candlelight and the tomb-like altars and the resonant corridors in their tall churches, but priests and servers triumphantly raised their voices as they stood beneath brilliantly coloured frescoes of scenes from biblical stories.

From the simple recitation of the psalms, chanting developed into extended lines of freely flowing melody. Singers no longer kept to one note for each syllable, but allowed their voices to rise and fall in an uninterrupted stream of sound on such singable words as 'Alleluia' or 'Amen'. Hundreds of melodies were invented. In the sixth century, Pope Gregory collected all the existing chants and arranged them in the order in which they are still sung every Sunday and saint's day in churches and cathedrals throughout the Roman Catholic world.

In their tall churches, the priests and servers raised triumphant voices as they stood beneath the brilliantly patterned frescoes and mosaics.
Courtesy Herder-Verlag, from J. Wilpert: 'Die römischen Mosaiken und Malereien der kirchlichen Bauten'

For medieval musicians in many lands, the Church's experimental notation made new tunes easier to learn and old ones less easily forgotten.
Municipal Library, Bergamo (Wellsfoto)

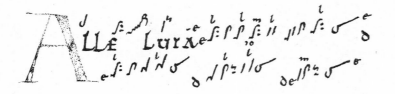

Neumes of the 10th-11th century: the ancestors of modern notation
Bodleian Library, Oxford

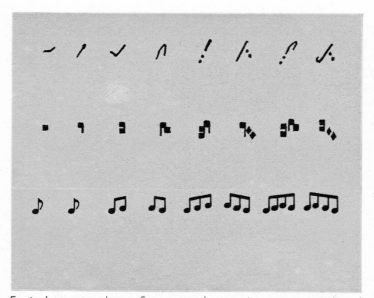

Equivalent notes shown, from top to bottom, in neumes, points and modern notation. Points are still used in printed books of plainsong.

By the end of the sixth century there were so many Gregorian chants that nobody could remember them all. These melodies, which we call plainchant, had to be written down. The Church's first experimental musical notation was a series of short curves which followed the rise and fall of the voices: the curves were called 'neumes' from the Greek word for signs. By the tenth century, a horizontal line was added, running from beginning to end of the chant, with a letter against it to show what level of pitch the line represented. This letter was called the clef, as it was the key to the position of the semitones. F and C were then the only letters used for clefs. In the eleventh and twelfth centuries, three more lines were added. These four parallel lines were called the 'staff' or 'stave'.

By this time musicians used written 'notes' instead of neumes. The notes, which were called 'points', were square. This was because of the way the monks copying the music used their quill pens. The notes were written either on the lines or in the spaces; for instance, the note on the line with the F clef in front of it was F; the note in the space above it was G and the note in the space below it was E. The clefs could be written on any line of the stave.

C_1 D_1 E_1 F_1 G_1 A_1 B_1 C D E F G A B c = c d e f g a b c^1 d^1 e^1 f^1 g^1 a^1 b^1 c^2

Modern notation: showing four octaves, from the low notes of the bass clef to the high notes of the treble clef. 'Middle C' is in both clefs.

Initial from the Book of Kells, designed by Irish monks, 7-800 A.D.
Trinity College, Dublin

Many monks were fine scholars and artists. They were great travellers too; carrying their art and learning throughout Europe.
National Gallery, London

This system of notation is not unlike the one we use today. We have added a fifth line to the stave. Our notes are now oval in shape, instead of square. The F clef, which was originally written $\digamma$ is now $\mathcal{9}$. It is always put on the fourth line from the bottom of the stave and it is called the bass clef because it is used for all lower voices and instruments. We still occasionally use the C clef, on the third or fourth line, for instruments of middle range, and we have added a third clef, the G clef. This was originally written $\mathcal{6}$, but it has now become transformed into $\mathcal{\&}$. The G clef is always written on the second line of the stave; it is called the treble clef because it is used for all higher voices and instruments. Musicians owe a debt of gratitude to the eleventh-century scholar Guido of Arezzo, who invented movable names for the steps or degrees of the scale. He took the first syllable of each line of a well-known hymn to St. John that happened to have a tune moving up one note higher on every phrase:

'UT-queant laxis,
RE-sonare fibris,
MI-ra gestorum,
FA-muli tuorum,
SOL-ve polluti,
LA-bii reatum.'

(That with easy voice Thy servants may be able to sing the wonders of Thy deeds, remove all sin from their polluted lips.)

The note UT was always the focal point of any tune; other notes were sung in relation to it.

This is the system on which our modern tonic-solfa is founded. It helped the monks of the Middle Ages to read unfamiliar chants on their journeys in foreign countries, and it lightened the task of those who spent the whole of their lives copying illuminated manuscripts of Gregorian plainchant.

Musicians owe much to Guido of Arezzo, a Benedictine monk born a thousand years ago.
National Library, Vienna

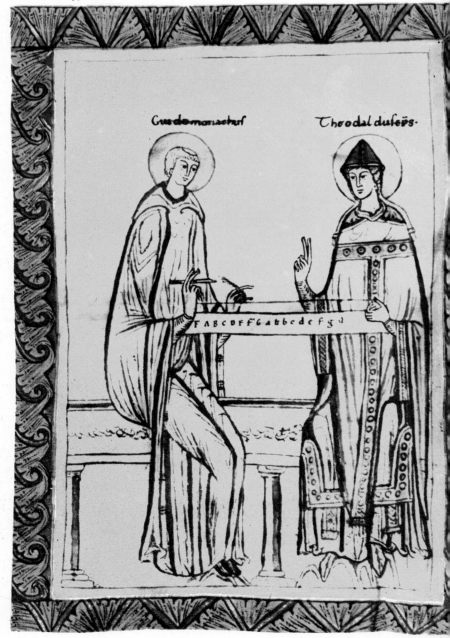

Overleaf: medieval manuscript of a hymn (c.1415)
British Museum

stella . dei mater alma . atqz

semp uurgo felix œli porta

13th-century notation of music sung in three-voice counterpoint

20th-century notation of part of the same music clearly shows the notes of the lowest voice stretched out in 'augmentation'.
Harvard University Press, after Apel: 'The Harvard Dictionary of Music'

Until the middle of the ninth century, church music had consisted of a single line of melody, sung by one voice or by a choir. Then, in about 850, groups of singers began to experiment with two notes at the same time, finding that the combined sound or 'interval', was more resonant.

Intervals are described as a second, a third, a fourth and so on – counting up the scale from the lower note to the upper note. The size of some of the intervals varies according to where the semitones occur: larger intervals are called major, smaller are called minor.

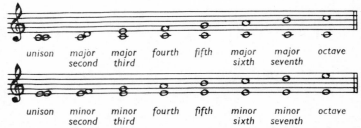

| unison | major second | major third | fourth | fifth | major sixth | major seventh | octave |

| unison | minor second | minor third | fourth | fifth | minor sixth | minor seventh | octave |

Some intervals are called dissonant; they sound so uncomfortable that we want the notes to move on somewhere else. Consonant intervals sound com-

Coutances Cathedral, France. The medieval Church was the great patron of all the arts.
Thames and Hudson, Bony & Hürlimann: ' French Cathedrals'

fortable. Octaves, fifths and fourths are perfect consonances; seconds and sevenths are dissonances. Somewhere between these are thirds and sixths: imperfect consonances. On a well-tuned piano we can hear the slight buzz of the thirds and sixths, and feel the discomfort of the seconds and sevenths.

In the ninth century people began singing plainchant in parallel motion in intervals a fourth or a fifth apart. Later they sang in oblique motion, with one voice holding the same note while the other voice went up or down, sometimes passing through all the different intervals, according to the shape of the melodic line of the plainchant.

In the eleventh century musicians made the important discovery of contrary motion, with one voice going up and the other voice coming down. This added a new dimension to the art of music; from then onwards voices became more and more independent in their relations with each other. In the twelfth century the music of 'note-against-note' (or counterpoint) changed from the freely flowing rhythm of plainchant to a rhythm with a regular pulse divided into twos or threes. This helped to keep the independent voice-parts together.

As counterpoint developed, a third voice was added, and then a fourth. A single line of a chant was taken as the foundation of the music: its notes were stretched out in 'augmentation' in the lowest voice, like a great supporting arch in a cathedral, while the upper voices sang the same melody in quicker notes, like the smaller arches of the cathedral windows.

In the thirteenth century musicians found that several voices could begin one after another on the same tune, imitating each other as we do today when we sing rounds. This was one of the most exciting discoveries in European music.

In all these experiments the medieval Church was the unrivalled patron of music, as of all the other arts. Each country produced its own school of composers, beginning with the great French composer Pérotin, whose magnificent four-voice counterpoint was first sung at the Cathedral of Notre Dame in Paris at midnight on Christmas Eve, 1190.

After the 13th century, musicians would often come in one after another on the same tune much in the same way as we sing a round today. (*Mansell-Anderson photograph of bas-relief by della Robbia*)

This 15th-century French tapestry shows music-making as a popular pastime among the nobles of Burgundy.

German National Museums, Nuremburg (Alfred Wolf)

In medieval France people sang also secular, or non-religious, music. Very little is known of the minstrels who went from one castle to another, entertaining the feudal households with their ballads. Nor do we know much about the jongleurs, or jugglers, who were musician – acrobats. Not one of the tunes they played has survived, as far as we know; for their music was not written down.

The troubadour Peire Rogier, as depicted by the artist of a 13th-century manuscript

Bibliothèque Nationale, Paris

The first secular songs to be written down were those of the troubadours and trouvères, who were aristocratic poet-musicians living in France in the twelfth and thirteenth centuries. Their songs were nearly always about the joys of spring or the unsurpassable beauty of their exquisite ladies:

Qant li ro-si-gnols s'es-cri-e Qui nos des du – it de son chant *etc.*

The fashion for these songs spread to other countries. The German troubadours were called minnesingers, 'Minne' meaning 'courtly love'.

Win-der wie ist nu dein Kraft Worden gar un – si-ge-haft

Seyt der Maye seinen schafft Auf dir hat zu-sto — chen. *etc.*

These songs were all written in the 'natural' scales or modes which can be found on the white notes of the piano. D to D, called the Dorian mode, was one of the most popular. Other modes were: C to C, Ionian; E to E, Phrygian; F to F, Lydian; G to G, Mixolydian; A to A, Aeolian. If a tune was too high or too low for a singer he could begin on

any note he liked and carry the whole tune to a different level. The shape of the transposed tune could be adjusted by raising any note a semitone higher with the help of a sharp (written ♯), or lowering it a semitone with the help of a flat (written ♭). These two signs are still used today. We have added a third sign, ♮ , called a natural; it is used for cancelling a ♯ or ♭ .

The troubadours and minnesingers kept to a single line of melody in their songs; but secular rounds were already being sung in the fourteenth century, the most famous being the English round 'Sumer is icumen in':

Buchner: 'Musical Instruments Through the Ages' (Illek & Paul)
Musician-acrobats were welcome at many courts throughout Europe.

Sumer is i – cu-men in,__ Lhude sing cu-cu,

Groweth sed and bloweth med, And springeth wode nu,

(★ = entry of new voice)

Sing cu — cu, *etc.*

The secular counterpoint of the Middle Ages helped to bring into being the new music of the Renaissance which reached its Golden Age in the middle of the sixteenth century.

This three-part madrigal was printed to be sung round a table.
Courtesy Shakespeare Association

Throughout Europe there were so many great composers writing in the sixteenth century, that it would take any present-day musician a long lifetime to get to know all their works.

The printing of music had been invented in the fifteenth century; and by the time of the Golden Age it was possible for ordinary people to sing counterpoint in their own homes. They used to sit round the table after a meal, often sharing one music-book between them, its pages printed so that each singer had the notes of his own part facing him. The contrapuntal songs they sang were called madrigals, which means that they were in the mother-tongue: the notes and rhythms of their interweaving lines of melody were often intricate; and there must have been frequent occasions when the singers lost their place and had to begin again.

It was considered a social disgrace not to be able to read music at sight, just as it was a disgrace not to know the steps of the fashionable dances of that time. Such dances were the Pavane, 'staide and grave'; the Coranto, 'full of sprightliness and vigour'; the Galliard, either lively or sober; and the Lavolta, a favourite with Queen Elizabeth I, in which the ladies were thrown up into the air and bounced about until they were dizzy in the head.

A Musical Entertainment': from the painting by Sebastian Florigerio
Alte Pinakothek, Munich

Musicians playing for a courtly dance in the Golden Age of music: one of the many fine engravings by the German artist, Theodor de Bry
British Museum

Many of the later madrigals were founded on dance-rhythms. In these short, cheerful part-songs the voices abandoned their independence and drew together on the main pulse of the music, keeping to a simple rhythm for the refrain of *FA la-la LA* at the end of each verse.

This dancing rhythm was one of the causes of an epoch-making change in music which happened in about the year 1600. Instead of listening horizontally to the long, interwoven threads of counterpoint, musicians began to listen vertically to the combined intervals they were singing. These combined intervals are called chords. Moving from one chord to another is harmony.

As soon as composers began writing music in harmony, rather than in counterpoint, they discarded the modal scales of the early church music and the troubadour songs, and wrote either in the C to C mode, which they called the major scale, or in a modified version of the A to A mode, called the minor scale.

Tunes founded on the notes of the C major scale are described as being in the 'key' of C. Music can be transposed into any key. For instance, a tune in C major can be written in G, with the addition of an F sharp to make the scale the right shape in tones and semitones. Or it could be written in F with the addition of a B flat.

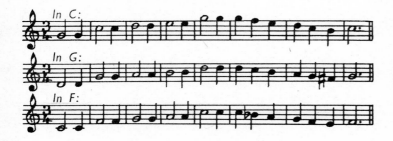

A device, called a key-signature, shows where the sharps or flats occur in each key.

The change-over from counterpoint to harmony had far-reaching effects on the whole of European music. One of the immediate results was that people gave up singing madrigals in their homes and preferred to sing to the accompaniment of instruments.

After 1600, people sang with instruments, in harmony.
Bibliothèque Nationale, Paris

Instruments and Players

Anything that sets up sound vibrations can become an instrument. A hollow tree can be hit with a stick: a hollow bamboo can be blown into: the trip-thong of a hunter's snare can be plucked. We can experiment with these jungle methods by tapping the surface of a table with a pencil, or blowing suddenly into the cap of a fountain-pen, or stretching a thin rubber band as far as it will go and twitching it with a finger or thumb.

Modern orchestral instruments are divided into three main categories: those that are hit are percussion instruments; those that are blown are wind instruments; those that can be plucked or scraped are string instruments. Within each main division there are family groups, each member having its own characteristic voice that is easy to recognise.

The characteristic sound of an instrument depends upon its shape and size, the materials out of which it is made, and the particular device that sets it vibrating. It also follows a law of acoustics which concerns the vibrations themselves. This law can be worked out mathematically. A string vibrates for its whole length. Simultaneously, it vibrates in sections of a half, a third, a quarter, and so on. Each of these vibrating sections produces a *very* faint note of its own, according to its own frequency: the shorter the section, the higher the frequency. These very faint notes are called overtones, or upper partials, or harmonics. The amplitude of the vibrations gets less and less as the vibrating sections get smaller and smaller, which means that the higher overtones can very seldom be heard as actual notes.

The frequencies of the harmonics are exact multiples of the frequency of the fundamental note of the whole vibrating length. If the frequency of the fundamental is x, the frequencies of the sections will be in the series 2x, 3x, 4x, etc. It is therefore possible to find the pitch of the harmonic series from any given fundamental note:

(Nos. 7 and 11 are slightly 'out of tune', that is, they are not at the normal level of pitch.) Some of these harmonics can be heard by playing No. 1 on the piano and holding the pedal down.

The character of every musical instrument—whether it is percussion, wind, or stringed – depends on how audible any of the harmonics are.

Ancient instrumentalists
carved on ivory c. 900 B.C.
British Museum

The Metropolitan Museum of Art, New York City
Egyptian instruments and players – a scene painted 3,400 years ago, showing the ancestors of some of our modern orchestral instruments

Indian banya drum,
played not with sticks but with fingers
Uday Shankar and Company

A Roman mosaic, showing an actor playing the 'tinkling cymbals' of 2,000 years ago
National Museum, Naples (Mansell-Anderson)

The chief percussion instrument is the drum. Its vibrating surface is a skin which is tightly stretched across the open ends of a hollow, resonant cylinder or broad tube. The greater the tension of the skin, the higher the pitch. In some countries – particularly India – a drummer's fingers know just where to find each sectional vibration for the harmonics.

In Western orchestras the drums are played with soft-headed sticks. Side-drums have pencil-thin sticks that make a brittle sound. Other modern percussion instruments are the triangle, which clinks; the tambourine, which jingles; and the castanets, that clack. Cymbals are large plates of Turkish brass clashed together: they are descendants of the small 'tinkling cymbals' of two thousand years ago. When a player holds up one cymbal and touches it with a soft-headed stick, it makes a bell-like sound.

Chiming bells in an orchestra are now tubular instead of bell-shaped: their overtones are so audible that they often sound like complicated chords. The gong is loud enough to drown all other orchestral notes. It must never be played too violently, for the sound is powerful enough to cross the threshold of pain, and could deafen a listener for life.

Grimsby Evening Telegraph
A modern drummer demonstrating his many instruments, including Chinese gong, side-drum, kettle-drums (or timpani) and tubular bells

Angel blowing trumpet: based
on a figure
from a medieval manuscript
National Library, Vienna

The only members of the orchestra that can compare in power with the percussion are the brass wind instruments. All the brass instruments consist of a long tube with a cupped mouthpiece. A player can get any note in the harmonic series by altering the pressure of his lips: the greater the pressure, the higher the harmonic. The familiar notes of a trumpet-call owe their brilliance to the clear, energetically produced harmonics. No other instrument can sound so triumphant, which is why so many pictures show angels playing long, golden trumpets at the gates of heaven.

Horns can also sound brilliant, though some of their most characteristic notes are in the mellow range of the lower harmonics. Primitive horns were made from the horns of animals. The noise they made must have sounded terrifying: it was the blast of rams' horns that was said to have flattened the walls of Jericho. The earliest direct ancestor of the orchestral horn was the medieval hunting-horn, which had its brass tube curled round and round so that the huntsman could slip one arm through it while riding, without any risk of it getting in the way. Ever since then horns have been this shape.

In modern orchestras the horns and trumpets are no longer limited to the 'open' notes of the harmonic series; they are able to get all the remaining notes with the help of three pistons, or valves, which let in extra bits of tube to lower the pitch when required.

Trombones do not need valves, as they have a separate length of tubing which slides in and out, enabling them to get all the notes they need. Trombones can be played as brilliantly as trumpets, but they can also sound solemn.

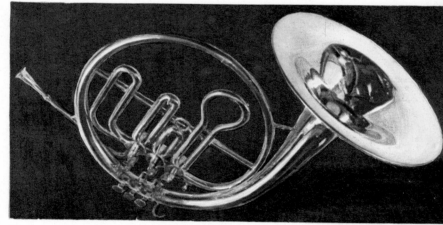

The valved horn can play more notes than its medieval ancestor.
After Buchner: 'Musical Instruments Through the Ages'

The modern trombone differs little from its predecessor,
the sackbut, or 'pull-push'.
Bibliothèque Nationale, Paris

Japanese transverse flute—near relation of the orchestral flute

Peruvian vessel designed in the form of a man playing a simple flute
British Museum (R. L. Jarmain)

Woodwind instruments are more gentle in sound than the brass. Gentlest of all is the flute. The primitive ancestor of the flute family was a one-note pipe made of bone or bamboo. The pitch of its note depended on the length of the pipe. When several pipes of different lengths were joined side by side, as in the instrument called the panpipes, it became possible to play tunes. A better way of getting different notes was discovered by taking a single pipe and boring holes at various distances along it. Each hole altered the length of the vibrating column of air in the instrument; so that the notes of a scale could be played by covering all the holes with the fingers and then lifting one finger after another. This is the method which is still used, though modern flutes have metal levers called 'keys' which cover the holes. The connecting mechanism of these keys makes it easier to play intricate fingering. The flute is held cross-wise: the player does not cover the mouth-hole but lets his breath strike the edge of it.

An end-blown flute, called the recorder, is a relation of the orchestral 'transverse' flute. A recorder player puts the instrument to his lips, and his breath is guided through a narrow slit towards the sharp edge of a window-shaped opening in the pipe. The recorder went out of fashion during the nineteenth century, but it was revived about fifty years ago and has recently become very popular in Europe and America, for it is the easiest wind instrument for beginners to learn.

Recorders—old instruments popular with young woodwind players in Europe and America
(Alfred Lammer)

Left: an ancient Etruscan wall-painting of reed-intruments played in pairs. Right: a present-day reed-instrument, the expressive oboe
Courtesy Editions Skira   *Terence Le Goubin*

A grass-blade, or reed, held between two thumbs and blown upon, will produce a shrill squawk. A reed, stuck into the end of a bamboo pipe, makes a primitive reed-instrument. It is the ancestor of our modern oboe, which can sound more expressive than any other woodwind instrument.

The ancient reed-instruments of the Egyptians, Greeks and Etruscans were often played in pairs. Instruments like these can still be heard in the Near and Far East; the sound they make carries to an astonishing distance. The earliest European reed-instruments were single pipes called shawms. They were used for open-air music in the courtyards and market-places: they are still played in parts of Spain. In the shawm band there were different-sized instruments, just as there are in the modern oboe family which includes the cor anglais and bassoon.

Present-day reed-instruments are all keyed, like flutes, but they still depend on the equivalent of a grass-stalk for their reeds. Special reed-cane is grown in the south of France for supplying most of the woodwind players in Europe. It has to be carefully dried, and great skill is needed in cutting it.

Oboes and bassoons have double reeds which vibrate against each other. The clarinet, which has evolved from the 'drone' of the bagpipes, has a single reed which vibrates against the wall of the pipe. The clarinet's lowest notes are dark, the middle notes are mellow, while the highest notes can sound like distant trumpets.

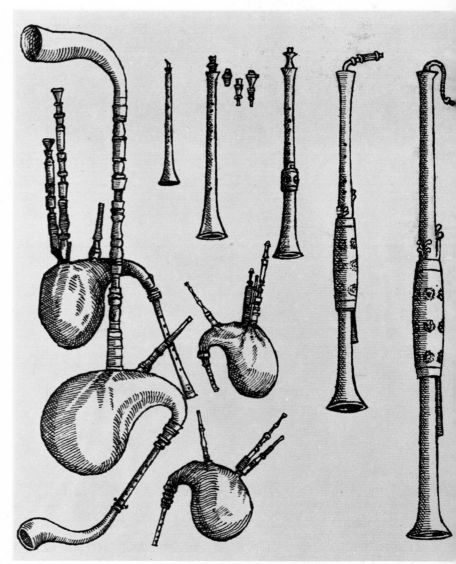

16th-century engraving of reed-instruments: bagpipes and shawms

The harp's history goes back 4,000 years. Here, a sambyke harp, cithara and lyre are depicted on a Greek vase well over 2,000 years old.
Museum antiker Kleinkunst, Munich (Hirmer Verlag)

Japanese samisen, one of many plucked instruments played in the East

*L. Hajek: 'Harunobu' (W. & B. Forman)
Original in National Gallery, Prague*

Of all the stringed instruments, the harp is probably the oldest that is still played. Each string of a harp has its own note: the longer the string, the lower the pitch. The Greeks played the harp; but their favourite stringed instrument was the lyre. The lyre's strings were all of the same length, but were strung at different tensions. Although the lyre had fewer strings than the harp, the player could get more notes by 'stopping' each string; by pressing it with a finger he shortened the string's vibrating length and raised its pitch.

Plucked instruments of many shapes are still played in all Eastern countries. The Arabian *al'ud* is the direct ancestor of the European lute – an instrument with a hollow pear-shaped body which was to be found in every musician's home during the sixteenth century. The lute provided a perfect accompaniment to a singer, for it could play chords as well as tunes and was so flexible that it could express the changing moods of a song. In spite of the lute's technical difficulties many amateurs learned to play it for their own delight; this proved an expensive hobby, for the tightly-stretched gut strings frequently broke and had to be renewed. Unfortunately there are very few twentieth-century lute players. But the guitar, a member of the same family, is still very popular among amateur players.

The lute, now seldom heard, was popular throughout 16th-century Europe.
The Academy, Venice (Foto Fiorentini photograph of painting by Carpaccio)

The first bowed instruments came from the East. Arabian craftsmen experimented with a Persian lute: instead of plucking it in the usual way they took an archer's bow and drew it to and fro across the strings. The scraping sound had musical possibilities. This bowed instrument was called the *rebab*, and it reached medieval Europe as the rebeck; it was the small fiddle that the jongleurs played.

European craftsmen soon improved the tone of their bowed instruments. They made them in different sizes, so that by the sixteenth century it was possible to play contrapuntal string music in several parts. The new instruments were called viols – the treble, alto, tenor and bass viol corresponding (though not very closely) to our violin, viola, cello and bass. Viols had a less brilliant tone than our modern instruments. Their bows were still slightly arched, and the tension of the hairs was less than ours, which made it easier to play chords. The small viols were usually held downwards, resting between the players' legs, instead of being held against their shoulders like violins.

The first genuine violins were made in Italy in the sixteenth and seventeenth centuries. The most famous makers were Nicolo Amati and his pupil Antonio Stradivari who made the best violins in the world. Violin makers still use their patterns. Their craft is highly skilled; and musicians owe a debt of gratitude to the generations of makers who have transformed wood and varnish and sheep's guts and horse-hair into expressive instruments capable of making such a variety of beautiful sounds.

Medieval rebecks, descendants of the Arabian rebab

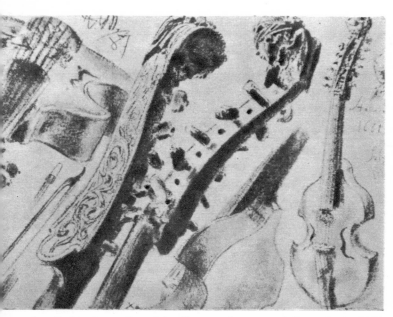
Pencil drawings of a viola d'amore (a tenor viol) made in 1661

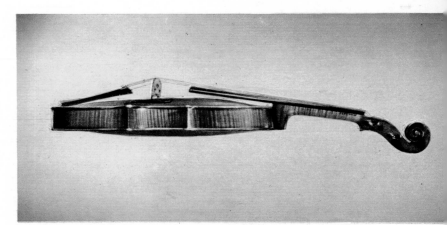
A 200-year-old Stradivari violin, unsurpassed by modern craftsmen
Victoria and Albert Museum, London (R. L. Jarmain)

A Roman hydraulis. Early organs resembled sets of giant panpipes.
National Museum, Naples

Greek engineers invented the first organ, an instrument with the name *hydraulis*, which resembled a large set of panpipes with a wind-supply worked by water-pressure. Each pipe could be connected to the wind-supply by a separate lever, called a key, which the player pressed down with his fingers.

From 400A.D. onwards the wind for this earliest of all keyboard instruments was provided by bellows. The sound of the early medieval organ must have been painfully raucous. A fifth-century organ in Jerusalem was said to have been heard a mile away at the Mount of Olives. In the tenth century there was a gigantic English organ which was played by two organists. It had four hundred pipes and twenty-six bellows worked by seventy strong men: a writer of the time reported that every listener held his hands over his ears while it was played, 'being in no wise able to draw near and bear the sound'.

In complete contrast were the small house-organs of the later Middle Ages: their delicate mechanism could be worked with one pair of hands at the bellows, and their soft notes resembled the sound of distant recorders.

Our modern organs, electrically blown, with pedals for the feet and four keyboards, or manuals, for the hands, are powerful enough to challenge an *hydraulis*. Hundreds of pipes enable the player to choose from a wide range of notes, from the lowest bass to the highest treble, and to vary the tone colour from the gentlest whisper of a flute to the full resonance of horns and trumpets and trombones.

By kind permission of the General Manager, Royal Festival Hall, London
The four keyboards, pedals and stops of a powerful modern organ

A small house-organ of the late Middle Ages, embroidered on a French tapestry
Cluny Museum, Paris (Giraudon)

The clavichord – earliest and quietest stringed keyboard instrument
Worcester Art Museum, Mass. (Barney Burstein)

The earliest stringed keyboard instrument is the clavichord, which dates from the fourteenth century. It is very simple in construction: when the keys are pressed down, the strings are gently touched by little brass wedges called tangents. The clavichord is so soft that it cannot be combined with other instruments, or voices. It is ideal for playing at home, as its expressive notes are so quiet that they are never overheard by next-door neighbours.

The harpsichord, dating from the sixteenth century, is powerful enough to be played with voices or other instruments. The resonant wooden case enclosing the strings is shaped like a horizontal harp. When the player's finger strikes a key, an upright bit of wood at the far end of the lever jumps towards the string and plucks it with a crow's quill. The tone of the harpsichord can vary from a delicate lute-like whisper to a brilliant sparkling sonority; for there are several strings to choose from for each note, and adjustments that can reduce the sound or augment it with upper or lower octaves.

Even on the most highly developed eighteenth-century harpsichord, it was not possible to change from loud to soft within one short phrase. This rapid change is a characteristic of the modern piano; it was called the *pianoforte*, because it can play both softly and loudly without extra machinery.

The strings of the piano are hit with felt-covered hammers. The modern instrument has a metal frame within its wooden case. This is to take the strain of the string tension which, in a full-sized grand piano, exerts a pressure of over twenty tons.

Deutsches Museum, Munich (Sophie-Renate Gnaman)
Hans Ruckers, the 'harpsichord Stradivari', made this 16th-century instrument. Its legs are later in date.

Courtesy Steinway and Sons
A craftsman tests a modern grand piano before it leaves the factory.

In a small group, each player is able to offer his own suggestions.
Château de Maisons-Laffitte (Yvan Pillonel photograph of painting by Leonello Spada)

Music-making in the home has flourished from the sixteenth century onwards. Amateur instrumentalists have an advantage over professionals. They can spend as long as they like over practising one piece of music, without worrying about anyone listening to them. In a small group, each player can offer his own suggestions as to whether a phrase should be quicker or slower, louder or softer: the playing may not always be perfectly in tune, and there may be uncomfortable moments when the rhythm is uneven, but after much perseverance the music gradually comes to life.

Amateurs who lived during the Renaissance were particularly fortunate, as they had so many great composers writing instrumental music for them to play. The most famous writers of chamber-music at the end of the sixteenth, and the beginning of the seventeenth century were the Englishmen, William Byrd, Orlando Gibbons and Thomas Morley (a friend of Shakespeare); the Dutch composer, Sweelinck; the Germans, Schein and Scheidt; and the Italians, Banchieri and Frescobaldi.

Sixteenth-century chamber-music was mostly played by groups of viols or recorders. The printed music for these 'consorts' seldom mentioned which instruments were to be used. The parts were described as 'first voice', or 'second voice'; and could be played on whatever instrument happened to be handy. If necessary, a part could be sung instead of played, because the music was 'apt for voices or viols'. Musicians often played short collections of dance-tunes, strung together to make a continuous whole. They also played contrapuntal fantasies, where the composer could use a tune according to his fancy, introducing it in close imitation, in quicker notes (*diminution*), slower notes (*augmentation*) or upside down (*inversion*). And they played Variations on a Ground, varying the notes of a well-known song or dance-tune and changing the mood from solemn to sprightly, while keeping to the same simple bass notes of the Ground; which were played over and over again on the bass viol.

16th-century brass consorts played on grand occasions. State trumpeters are here seen at the funeral of Charles V, Holy Roman Emperor.

Large groups of instruments needed someone to keep them together. Here the composer is directing from the harpsichord.
Bavarian State Library, Munich

Brass instruments were unsuitable for chamber-music as they were too loud to be played in a small room: they belonged to open-air processions in the streets or to festive occasions in cathedrals or in spacious banqueting halls.

Towards the end of the sixteenth century, composers began combining different groups of instruments in the same piece of music. In their extended choral works they placed brass, woodwind and strings in the different galleries of a cathedral, alternating the groups for contrasts of loud and soft music. On other occasions a composer would gather all his singers and instrumentalists around him and would direct them from the harpsichord.

The Venetian composer Andrea Gabrieli was the first to combine voices and instruments in this way on a grand scale. His influence spread throughout Europe, for he was a great teacher as well as a great composer. His nephew, Giovanni Gabrieli, can be called the founder of the orchestra, for he was the first composer to indicate in his printed copies the exact instruments he wanted for each part.

Drama in Music

The golden age of Renaissance music coincided with a golden age of drama: but it was not until the end of the sixteenth century that anyone thought of bringing the two arts together. Music in a Shakespeare play is incidental. There are fanfares of trumpets for the approach of a king, drum-rolls for a funeral, dances for a wedding and songs sung to the lute during a love scene: but no one would have thought of trying to sing the words of the dramatic dialogues or the poetic soliloquies.

In about the year 1600 several Italian poets, artists, actors and musicians met together in a Florentine palace to discuss the possibility of creating a musical style similar to what they imagined the choruses in Greek tragedy might have sounded like. This was the beginning of opera.

The scripts, or *libretti*, were specially written to be set to music; their dramatic subjects were taken from Greek legends. Actors abandoned the wide apron stages of the sixteenth-century theatre and concentrated their gestures within the framework of a proscenium arch. Costumes and settings were pastoral or heroic in character, and the music was a sung declamation, called recitative, which followed the natural rhythm of the spoken word.

Recitative was accompanied by a harpsichord and a bass viol. The composer wrote the bass notes of the accompaniment and added numerical figures in a kind of musical shorthand to show what chords were to be played. Each figure given with the bass note represented an interval above that note: for instance, in the key of C, if C were the given bass note, $\frac{5}{3}$ indicated the chord CEG, (C=1, E=3, G=5), while $\frac{6}{3}$=CEA, $\frac{6}{4}$=CFA, and so on. If sharps or flats that were not in the key-signature were needed, they were written after the figure.

The notes of a chord could be spaced in any order above the bass note, and there was no need to play them simultaneously: they could be spread out slowly, or broken up into harp-like cascades called arpeggios to add to the dramatic effect of the singer's words in the recitative.

In this kind of accompaniment, called 'figured bass', the keyboard player was free to improvise his own part as he went along, provided that he kept to the right chords. While realising the composer's intentions he could also follow the singer's gestures, and give him sympathetic and flexible support in all the changing moods of his song.

Oxford University Press, Dr. Towneley Worsthorne : 'Venetian Opera in the Seventeenth Century'   *(Mansell-Anderson)*

The Italian inventors of opera owed a great deal of their inspiration to the arts and architecture of both classical Greece and Rome.

The first outstandingly great composer of opera was Claudio Monteverdi, who lived and worked in Venice in the early seventeenth century. He used exciting instrumental accompaniment in his operatic songs, which were called 'arias', and he developed the harmonies of his figured basses so that he could convey any mood of the drama with a few chords.

Opera was brought into France by a young Florentine composer called Lully, who became a naturalised Frenchman and a court musician to Louis XIV. He reached Paris at a time when French craftsmen were improving the tone of woodwind instruments; and it is in his operas that the oboe, which takes its name from *hautbois*, first became an expressive solo instrument.

Ballets were then the fashion in Paris; and by introducing a large number of dances into his pastoral operas, Lully became a popular success as a composer. He was himself an actor and a dancer. He invented the Minuet, which was said to be the French king's favourite dance. He also collaborated with Molière, the famous writer of comedies, in ballets and *divertissements*. Lully was one of the first composers to write music that was founded on the modified version of the Aeolian mode, which we now call the harmonic minor scale:

Opera reached England in the second half of the seventeenth century, when the stage entertainments called Masques were becoming transformed into

Claudio Monteverdi (1567–1643), greatest of the early opera composers

Scene showing dancers performing in an opera by Jean Baptiste Lully (1632–1687), himself a ballet dancer and the inventor of the Minuet

SOLO. *A single* **SONG.**

¡Ark! hark! the ecch'ing Air a tri- - - - - - - -umph sings, hark! the

The beginning of a song by Henry Purcell (1659–1695), a great English composer with a genius for 'expressing the energy of English words'
National Portrait Gallery, London

dramatic works with continuous music. The great English opera composer was Henry Purcell. He had an astonishingly keen sense of the musical possibilities of his native language. His settings of descriptive adjectives, such as 'triumphant', or 'drooping', are so vivid that they almost convey actual gestures. He could take a word and repeat it over and over again, adding new life to it and making it sound more and more important at each repetition. He gave the characters in his dramas a musical personality that was subtler and more distinctive than anything the spoken libretto could give them.

Purcell died at the age of thirty-six, having written incidental music for fifty plays, as well as the opera *Dido and Aeneas*, which is his masterpiece.

In Italy the operatic tradition begun by Monteverdi was continued in the late seventeenth and early eighteenth centuries by the Neapolitan composer Alessandro Scarlatti and his son Domenico. Alessandro has been described as the originator of *bel canto*, a singing technique that emphasises beauty of tone and brilliance of performance, and which has remained an ideal for many opera singers.

Italy was considered to be the centre of musical life during the eighteenth century. Throughout Europe, the very words describing the speed at which a piece of music should be performed were written in Italian. We still use such words as *Allegro*: quick; *Vivace*: lively; *Presto*: very quick; *Andante*: gently moving; *Largo*: broadly; *Adagio*: slow. Other frequently used Italian words are *crescendo*: getting louder; *diminuendo*: getting softer; *accelerando*: getting quicker; *rallentando*: getting slower; *legato*: smoothly; *staccato*: detached.

National Library, Turin
Sketch for the set of an opera by Domenico Scarlatti (1685–1757)

Liceo Musicale, Bologna
Alessandro Scarlatti (1660–1725), wrote the music for 100 operas.

The most famous eighteenth-century composer of Italian opera was Handel, who was born in Germany and later naturalised as an Englishman. He spent a great deal of his life travelling and must have felt at home in any country in Europe. He had met Domenico Scarlatti in Rome when they were both in their early twenties, and had been fired with enthusiasm for the *bel canto* of the Neapolitan school.

Handel wrote more than forty operas. Not many of them are performed today – partly because of the technical difficulties of some of the vocal writing. Many of his operas called for highly elaborate scenery and stage-effects; in his stage-directions we find statues rising from a trap-door surrounded by fire, while cupids fly about in mid air. Many eighteenth-century operatic conventions now seem pointless. One, which was rigidly observed throughout Handel's life, was that after a solo aria the singer must immediately go off into the wings. This meant that when the hero had proposed to the heroine he

An elegant 18th-century title-page for Handel's most famous work

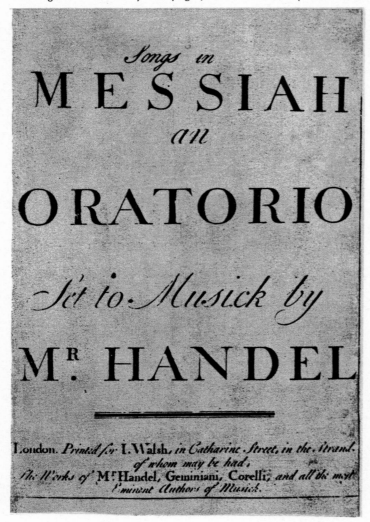

George Frideric Handel (1685–1759) – a contemporary oil-painting
State and University Library, Hamburg (Alf Schreyer)

had to walk off and leave her without waiting for her answer. Composer and librettist had to put up with this absurd situation, because the performers insisted on having an opportunity for prolonged applause at the end of every song. Opera singers were the popular stars of their time – and they could be very temperamental, especially during rehearsals.

Although Handel's operas are largely forgotten, his oratorios are still frequently performed, particularly his *Messiah*. An oratorio is like a religious opera but without action or scenery or costumes: all the drama is concentrated in the music. In Handel's oratorios there are amazingly dramatic moments, such as the scene in *Samson* where the recitative is suddenly interrupted by frantic scale passages in the orchestra, which give a vivid impression of the collapse of the Temple and the destruction of the crowd of Philistines.

Sudden dramatic changes of harmony could be achieved in eighteenth-century music as a result of

A painting of an Italian opera rehearsal, about 1710. Opera singers, the stars of their day, were often temperamental before a performance.
Courtesy Mrs. Leonard Messel, M.B.E. (R. L. Jarmain)

Sketch of Senesino and Faustina, two 18th-century opera singers
Reproduced by gracious permission of Her Majesty The Queen

A contemporary etching of Handel directing one of his oratorios
British Museum

the invention of a new system of tuning keyboard instruments. Before this, scales had been tuned so that each interval could be represented by a simple numerical ratio, such as 2 / 1 (octave), 3 / 2 (fifth), 4 / 3 (fourth), and so on.

This system of tuning was unsatisfactory for changes of key, because the pitch of the scale degrees would have had to be altered to keep the intervals in the right relation to the new UT or key-note. The new system of tuning, called 'equal temperament', is the one we still use. It divides the octave into twelve equal semitones, which means that every interval except the octave is very slightly out of tune.

The actual level of pitch of any given note has changed very often during the last few hundred years. Handel's middle C was lower than ours. Today all keyboard instruments have to be tuned so that c^1 (the octave above middle C) is equal to 523 vibrations per second.

The following table shows the frequencies of the equal-tempered semitones in the octave from c to c^1. (The frequency of the octave above any given note is always double the frequency of the note itself, so that with the help of these figures it is easy to calculate the frequency of any note on the piano.) c:261·1; c♯ or d♭:277·2; d:293·7; d♯ or e♭:311·1; e:329·6; f:349·2; f♯ or g♭:370; g:392; g♯ or a♭: 415·3; a:440; a♯ or b♭:466·2; b:493·9; c^1:523·2

Although Handel travelled so much he never met his famous German contemporary, Bach, who was the greatest of all writers of dramatic religious music.

Bach was born into a large family of hard-working musicians: he must have heard music all day long while still in his cradle. As a young man he studied the instrumental music of the Italian composer Vivaldi, rewriting his string orchestral works so that they could be played on the harpsichord. He also learned a great deal from the music of the Scandinavian composer Buxtehude: on one occasion he walked two hundred miles in order to listen to Buxtehude playing the organ.

Bach lived in Germany all his life, earning his living as a provincial organist and choirmaster. The works, called cantatas, which he wrote for his Sunday services, were like oratorio on a small scale. They usually began with a chorus, with orchestral accompaniment, founded on a familiar Lutheran hymn-tune. This would be followed by a solo aria, with a violin or flute or oboe adding its own melodic line. This instrumental part was called *obbligato* because it was essential to the music. (There is an example of an oboe obbligato to a bass aria in the facsimile of Bach's handwriting at the beginning and end of this book.) The arias in a cantata were linked by short recitatives; and the work ended with a straightforward version of the hymn-tune in which the congregation could sing with the choir.

The congregation also joined in the hymns throughout Bach's settings of the Passion. The tenor

Johann Sebastian Bach (1685–1750) – an oil-painting by Haussmann

St. Thomas's Church, Leipzig, where Bach became organist-choirmaster in 1723, and where he directed his own music for twenty-seven years

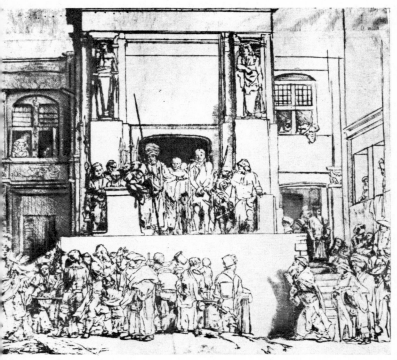

The Passion music of Bach is as dramatic as a Rembrandt etching.
Courtesy Phaidon Press and British Museum

A performance of church music, such as Bach must have directed

soloist sang the words of the Evangelist in dramatic recitative, describing each incident in the story, and leading up to the direct quotations of the words of Christ or Pilate which were sung by other solo voices. The chorus represented the crowds: in the angry scenes outside the judgment-hall their loud interjections and argumentative comments were as dramatic as the gestures of one of Rembrandt's pictures of the Gospel story.

The counterpoint in these crowd scenes, as in much of Bach's music, was in a style called 'fugal', which meant that the voices followed each other in close imitation, just as an idea passes from person to person in a crowd.

Bach was the first composer to write equal-tempered keyboard music in every major and minor key. When moving from one key to another, which is described as 'modulating', he often made use of an expressive four-note chord with each note three semitones apart – for example Fsharp A C Eflat.

If you play these notes on the piano, and then move the E flat down a semitone it leads to the key of G. Go back to Fsharp A C Eflat and move the C down a semitone; it leads to the key of E, for the E flat will have transformed itself into D sharp. This change, called 'enharmonic', was not invented by Bach; but he was the first composer to make frequent use of it to enrich the drama of his music.

Example of fugal counterpoint from the 'St. John Passion' by Bach

Styles in Music

When Bach died in 1750 his music was already considered to be out of fashion. His own sons were no longer satisfied with composing fugues: their father had been writing them superbly for nearly half a century and they felt the time had come for a change. They revered his music and his memory, but they knew that as young composers they must explore the new music that was being written and find their own way about in it. So they broke away from harmonic counterpoint and began writing in a new style.

There is no such thing as a straight path of progress in music, beginning in some remote, primitive past and stretching onward and upward towards some far-distant perfection. Instead, the history of music moves up and down and to and fro, with unexpected changes of style, as in any other art.

These changes can be seen particularly clearly in architecture, where styles can alternate between highly decorated and severely plain. New fashions in clothes can coincide with a complete change of style in dancing; which means that there will also be a change of style in music, since dancing and music are inseparably linked together.

The high, white wigs and the rigidly wired skirts of the late eighteenth century made it necessary for the ladies who wore them to hold their heads up stiffly when curtseying their way through the formal patterns of a Minuet. But in the nineteenth century, crinolines were softer and more pliable; while ringlets hung from shapely heads that were free to droop over one shoulder or turn from side to side in the graceful movements of a Waltz.

The far-reaching change that took place in the style of music in about 1750 was largely the result of a change in musical patronage. For hundreds of years the Church had been the chief patron of musicians. But Bach was the last of the great composers who managed to earn his living in the whole-time employment of church authorities.

The new patrons were the rich princes and land-owners who liked to have a resident composer working for them so that they and their guests could enjoy listening to music every evening. They employed their own orchestras of skilled instrumentalists, and sometimes built their own small opera-houses, for private performances of chamber operas. These connoisseurs wanted courteous formality in music; so their composers evolved new styles for them - *galant*, elegant and unruffled.

The Minuet – a stately dance well suited to 18th-century formality of fashion
Hulton Picture Library

The Waltz, with its freedom of movement, came into fashion with less formal clothes, and remained the 19th century's most popular dance.
British Museum

Franz Joseph Haydn (1732–1809), and the palace of Prince Nicholas of Esterházy, Haydn's patron

The first of the great composers to write music in the late eighteenth-century style was Haydn. As a young student in Vienna he had studied the works of one of Bach's sons, and had taught himself to write in the new classical sonata form. This meant using contrasting tunes, breaking them up into fragments, tossing the fragments to and fro, passing through one key after another, working up to a climax of suspense; and then returning to the original opening in its straightforward simplicity, with a tail-piece or coda, to show that the musical journey was at an end.

Haydn was employed on the country estate of the Esterházy family, where he spent thirty years in the Prince's household, writing and rehearsing and performing music for the enjoyment of the guests, and providing whatever kind of entertainment was required; he even wrote the tunes for the musical clocks that chimed the hours in the state apartments. In his chamber-music he made use of whatever instrumentalists were available, and soon discovered that the combined sound of two violins, a viola and a cello was just right for the new form, with its many possibilities for intimate musical conversations. This was the birth of the string quartet.

Mozart, the greatest of all the eighteenth-century classical composers, said that it was from Haydn that he first learned the true way to compose quartets. Mozart had been an infant prodigy. He was famous throughout Europe, not only as a composer but also as a performer on the newly-invented pianoforte. But in spite of this he was never able to earn an adequate living, for he insisted on working independently, without regular patrons. His father, who was a violin teacher, tried to persuade him to take pupils, but the twenty-two-year-old Mozart refused, saying: 'I am a composer and I neither can nor ought to bury the talent with which God in his goodness has so richly endowed me. I may say so without conceit, for I feel it now more than ever.'

All the same, his success with audiences was often great, and tunes from his operas were whistled through the streets of half-a-dozen capital cities of Europe. Best of all, his fellow-musicians recognised his genius. An eye-witness account of the first performance of his opera *Figaro* describes how the members of the orchestra went on and on applauding the composer, 'beating the bows of their violins against the music desks'.

With the fame of Haydn and Mozart, Vienna became the capital of the musical world and attracted a young German composer from Bonn. This was Beethoven, whose genius allowed his dynamic emotions to break the hitherto unruffled surface of late eighteenth-century music.

The eighteenth century had already come to an end by the time another Viennese, Schubert, began composing. Like Mozart, Schubert chose to work without any regular patron, and refused to spend

A title-page of quartets by Mozart, dedicated to his friend Haydn
Collection Aloys Mooser

Wolfgang Amadeus Mozart (1756–1791), at about the age of 13
Original in Mozart Museum, Salzburg

his time teaching in a school. As a result, he had a hard struggle to earn enough money to live on. One of his best-known works, the Trio in E flat for violin, cello and piano, brought him only a couple of hundred pence in payment. Schubert's music was seldom performed in public during his short life-time; but poets, painters and musicians used to crowd into a small room, week after week, to hear him accompany his friend Vogl in the songs he had just been writing, for they knew that 'everything he touched turned to music'.

Historisches Museum der Stadt Wien (Schubert-Museum)
His friends gathered week after week to hear Franz Schubert (1797–1828) accompany Vogl in the songs that he had just finished composing

At a Handel festival of a hundred years ago, London's Crystal Palace held an orchestra of 400; a chorus of 2,000; an audience of 20,000.

Nineteenth-century music is often called 'romantic' – a difficult word to define. To the German poets and musicians of the early nineteenth century it meant escape from the ordinary every-day world, into what they imagined the Romanesque world of the twelfth century might have been like, with its troubadours and minstrels, its knights in armour and ladies in tall, pointed hats, and its dark forests and high-towered castles. The first flowering of pure romantic music was the opera *Der Freischütz* by the German composer, Carl Maria von Weber, which has a scene of magic and horror in the Wolf's Glen.

Throughout most of the century, piano pieces were written with descriptive titles such as *Early Morning in Spring*, *The Haymakers*, or *Forest Murmurs*. These pieces were practised by solitary piano pupils – a complete contrast to music-making in the home in earlier centuries, when everyone had taken it for granted that amateur music was an occupation to be shared with other people.

Professional combined music-making was on a very much larger scale than ever before: huge choirs and orchestras of over a thousand performers gathered together in vast concert-halls. Solo in-

Hungarian Magnates are here presenting Liszt with a 'Sword of Honour' (from a cartoon).
Faber and Faber, Sacheverell Sitwell: 'Liszt'

Orchestral music by Berlioz, as it impressed a cartoonist in 1846
Faber and Faber, Sacheverell Sitwell: 'Liszt'

strumentalists were now the famous stars. The works they played with orchestral accompaniment, called concertos, had little in common with the chamber-concertos of Mozart or of Bach, where a soloist used to sit in the middle of a small group of instrumentalists, often sharing a music-stand with the player sitting next to him.

Nineteenth-century *virtuoso* performers, such as the violinist Paganini or the pianist-composer Liszt, were placed well in front of the ordinary members of the orchestra; and the works they played gave them frequent opportunity for displaying their unrivalled technical powers. Rapturous crowds followed them wherever they went, carrying them triumphantly through the streets of European capitals or strewing thousands of rose-petals at their feet.

The form of the music they played was still recognisable as having been adapted from the eighteenth-century classical sonata form of the Viennese school. But the mood of courteous formality was now transformed into a warmth that expressed the composer's personal emotions.

More and more use was made of the semitones between the notes of the major and minor scales, a device called 'chromaticism'. Earlier composers, including Bach and Purcell, had used chromatic

harmonies in their music. But nineteenth-century composers sometimes wrote long passages where every note of every chord moved chromatically: you can try this effect on the piano by playing the chord DFB and then moving it down in semitones for a whole octave. Keyboard instruments are particularly well designed for playing chromatic scale passages, because all the notes that make the semitones are already lying comfortably under the player's fingers.

Chromaticism led to the change of construction of brass instruments; and by the middle of the century horns and trumpets were fitted with valves which enabled them to play chromatic scales. This influenced the size and texture of the orchestra. Many more string players were added to balance the weight of the brass – who were now able to play throughout a whole piece, instead of having to limit themselves to passages that were founded on the open notes of the harmonic series. One of the results of this was that musical climaxes were very much louder than they had ever been before.

Opera singers now had to contend with a much more powerful orchestra. They needed to be physically tough to endure the strain of having to sing, for the best part of three hours, against the sustained resonance and the passionate outbursts of their orchestral accompaniment.

Victoria and Albert Museum, London (R. L. Jarmain)
Opera-houses like this were rebuilt to hold even bigger audiences

WOODWIND

Piccolo

Flutes, I, II

Oboes, I, II

Cor anglais
(English horn)

Clarinets I, II
in A

Bassoons I, II

BRASS

I, II
Horns in F
III, IV

Cornets I, II
in A

Trumpets I, II
in A

Tenor trombones I, II

Bass trombone
Tuba

PERCUSSION

Timpani

Triangle

Cymbals

Bass-drum

STRINGS

1st Violins

2nd Violins

Violas

Cellos

Double basses

A fragment from Tchaikovsky's full score of 'The Sleeping Beauty'

The full orchestra of today is still about the same size as that of 1900. Printed copies of orchestral music, called 'full scores', show the notes of all the different instruments, one above the other. The piccolo – a small flute – is fingered in the same way as the flute, but sounds an octave higher than it is written. The first flute and the second flute are marked I and II; they sometimes have a part each, and sometimes play in unison. This applies to all the woodwind marked I and II.

The flute's low notes are the quietest on the instrument; but the oboe gets louder as it goes down. The cor anglais is a larger-sized oboe, and is played by an oboist: it is called a transposing instrument because it is written a fifth higher than it sounds. This enables the oboist to use the same fingering whichever instrument he is playing.

Clarinets are also transposing instruments, for the same reason: they are either in B flat, written a tone higher than they sound, or in A, written a tone and a half higher than they sound. If the key of a work is D major, composers write for clarinets in A rather than in B flat, because players prefer the written key of F (one flat) to the written key of E (four sharps.) Bassoons are like bass oboes held diagonally, with an extra bit of tube for the mouthpiece.

Horns are transposing instruments; they are most often in F, written a fifth higher than they sound. They are used in two pairs: I and III taking the higher notes, and II and IV the lower. (Cornets are now rare in orchestras.) Trumpets were once transposing, but are now usually written as they sound.

⟍⟍				*getting louder*	
⟋⟋				*getting softer*	
p	soft	**mp**	*fairly soft*	**pp**	very soft
f	loud	**mf**	*fairly loud*	**ff**	very loud
>P	accented	‾P	sustained	·P	detached
♫	smooth	ᵛ	up-bow	⊓	down-bow
♫	marked	⌢	pause	‖: :‖	repeat

Some of the musical symbols which all instrumentalists must know

The full orchestra remains much the same size as it was in 1900. This photograph shows members of a modern Swiss orchestra rehearsing.
Jean Schneider, Lucerne

The tenor trombones are written in the C clef, with middle C on the fourth line of the stave. The one bass trombone often shares a stave with the tuba, which is a large, somewhat unwieldy instrument, like a bass horn with a mellow, cushiony tone.

Orchestral drums, called timpani, can be tuned to whatever notes the composer wants. Modern timpani have a pedal adjustment to enable them to alter their pitch very quickly. The most frequently used percussion instruments are bass-drum, side-drum and cymbals.

The strings are the only section of the orchestra where there are many players to each part. The leading violinist, violist and cellist are sometimes given a short solo, but they are usually in unison with their fellow players. The second violins play a different part from the firsts, but on the same sort of instrument, with the four strings tuned to G d a e^1. Violas play in the C clef, with middle C on the third line of the stave: their strings are tuned to C G d a. The cellos' strings are tuned an octave lower than those of the violas. Double basses have their strings tuned in fourths, E_1 A_1 D G. Their part is written an octave higher than it sounds, to avoid having too many notes below the stave, on the short lines called leger lines.

These are the normal instruments in a full orchestra. Composers add other percussion instruments, as well as harps and bass clarinets and double bassoons, whenever they want them.

East and West

Listening for the first time to an Indian musician singing or playing, a musician of the West is more than likely to feel bewildered; for the sound is utterly different from anything he has heard before. The tone seems harsh and the notes slide up and down in a manner that would never be tolerated in Europe or America. But the Indian musician may be just as bewildered by Western music. He will certainly be shocked by the out-of-tune division of the octave into twelve equal semitones.

The seven notes of the Indian scale are called by the Sanskrit syllables SA RE GA MA PA DHA NI (corresponding to our UT RE MI FA SOL LA SI), but of these notes only SA and PA remain at the same pitch, whatever the tune may be. The other scale degrees are flattened or sharpened according to what mode the music is in. If SA is C, MA can be either of two possible levels of F, or it can be one of four possible levels of F sharp. For instance, the modal scale C D E flat F sharp G A flat B C needs a sharper F sharp and a flatter A flat than we have in our equal-tempered notes of the modern keyboard instrument.

The single melodic line of Indian music is never harmonised with chords: it is accompanied by elaborate drum-rhythms which Europeans find exciting to listen to but difficult to follow. It is only after getting rid of all set notions of what music ought to sound like, that the Western listener can accept Indian music with an open ear.

One of the most obvious differences between Eastern and Western music is the way in which it is

A Kangra painting: 'The Festival of Spring'. Eastern painting and music may at first seem strange to those who are used to Western arts.
Victoria and Albert Museum, London (R. L. Jarmain)

presented. In a Western orchestra performers are placed on a platform in front of straight rows of listeners: they spend several minutes tuning their instruments: they open their printed copies of music at the right page: the conductor walks on to the platform to a loud burst of applause: he raises his baton; and the concert begins.

In India the performers sit cross-legged on the floor in the small space left by the semi-circle of listeners who are also sitting cross-legged on the floor. The drummer may take half an hour to get his instrument in tune; no one is impatient, for this is part of the ceremony of music-making. There are no written notes; for the music gradually emerges as an improvisation. There is no clapping, for it is considered 'barbarous'; but at an exciting climax or a subtly-turned phrase in the music the members of the audience show their obvious delight.

W. Suschitzky
The unhurried informality of these Indian players is in striking contrast with most performances of serious music in the Western World.

Eastern music has its roots in ceremony. Chinese music has traditions that can be traced back for at least four thousand years, when the sacred gong, called *huang chung*, gave the correct pitch to which all other instruments were tuned. Instruments were divided into eight traditional categories according to the materials they were made of; and each instrument was related to a point of the compass, a season of the year and an aspect of nature:

1	stone	N.W.	late autumn	sky
2	metal	W.	autumn	dampness
3	silk	S.	summer	fire
4	bamboo	E.	spring	thunder
5	wood	S.E.	early summer	wind
6	skin	N.	winter	water
7	gourd	N.E.	early spring	mountain
8	clay	S.W.	late summer	earth

In the T'ang Dynasty (618–907 A.D.) ceremonial music was performed by orchestras of three hundred players. The tunes they played were founded on a five-note (pentatonic) gapped scale without any semitones. You can try it out on the 'black notes' of the piano, and you will be surprised at the number of different tunes these five notes can make, especially if you vary the shape of the pentatonic scale by beginning on a different note.

Very little of the ceremonial music of China has survived to the present day. But some Chinese traditions have been preserved in the court and temple music of Japan. This music is played on a small

Chinese Deva with drum. Each instrument has its own significance.

Chinese orchestra: T'ang dynasty painting, over a thousand years old

An actor in ritual dress performing a Japanese Nō play – a ceremonial theatrical entertainment which has flourished for a thousand years
Koon Bunka Lab., Tokyo

Ministry of Education and Culture of the Republic of Indonesia
A section of the percussion instruments from a Balinese orchestra

orchestra of flutes, shawms, lutes, drums, gongs and a kind of mouth-organ called *shō* which has a cluster of reed-pipes sticking out of a gourd-shaped bowl. Traditional Japanese music also includes the dramatic chanting of the *Nō* plays – a ceremonial form of theatrical entertainment which has existed for at least a thousand years and is still performed today.

The most exciting traditional orchestras in the Far East are the *gamelan* orchestras of Java and Bali. They consist of a number of percussion instruments – rather like an orchestra of xylophones – made of different materials such as bamboo, wood, stone and bronze. Each of these instruments is tuned to the pentatonic scale. The largest instruments play the slowest notes; the smallest instruments play very fast, complicated patterns round the five notes of the scale on which the whole of the music is founded.

This elaborately organised variety which grows out of a few simple notes is the main characteristic of Eastern music. When an Indian singer and his drummer begin to improvise they are not plunging into the unknown and trusting to luck that they will keep together. They are starting with a given *raga*, which is a fixed melodic formula appropriate to a particular time of the day and season of the year, and they develop it according to tradition, sometimes taking two or three hours over it, offering suggestions to each other and working up to tremendous climaxes with the freedom of confidence.

'Janosik with his band': a Slovakian folk-painting of musicians whose vitality may owe as much to the gypsies as to their own folk-tunes
Artia: Slovak Folk Art (Alex Paul)

It was in the nineteenth century that Western composers first took any real interest in Eastern music. They were beginning to think about national characteristics in music and were exploring the folk-songs of their own countries and introducing them into their works. Russian composers, who used folk-music from Central Asia and Asia Minor, were among the first to write in a deliberately national style. When Central European countries followed their example, they found that their own folk-songs had often got mixed up with the music of the gypsies, so that in a good many cases it was difficult to tell which was which.

No one knows for certain where the gypsies came from. They were an Indian race, travelling from east to west, bringing with them their own language but borrowing almost everything else from the country they were passing through. The gypsies used an Indian scale, C D flat E F G A flat B C, for rhythmic incantations in their fortune-telling, and when they borrowed Rumanian, Hungarian and Slavonic folk-tunes for their songs and dances they adapted them to their own style, using flamboyant flourishes that belonged more to the East than to the West. This particular style suited the violin better than any other instrument. Gypsy violinists became internationally famous: Haydn heard them when they were invited to Esterházy, and Schubert listened to them while sitting with his friends in the cafés of Vienna. Later in the nineteenth century, several composers, including Liszt and Brahms, wrote Rhapsodies founded on gypsy violinists' versions of Central European tunes.

In Spain the gypsies found folk-tunes that were already Eastern in origin. The Moors had brought their own musical scales as well as their musical instruments into Spain, and their traditions never died out: the songs we now describe as 'flamenco' are still sung with their opening words in Arabic.

Flamenco has become popular in the United States of America, where the national music has grown from traditional European tunes and, in particular, from the folk-music of Africa.

When the Civil War was over, groups of negroes travelling from one small town to another attracted crowds of listeners when they sang their 'spiritual' songs, adapting the harmonies they had heard during missionary services. There was a deep melancholy in their singing, which coloured their descriptions of crossing the river Jordan and of the long journey over the desert to the Promised Land.

The negroes also sang work-songs while picking cotton in the field or working on the railroads: these were later transformed into American 'shouts', 'walk-arounds' and 'field-hollers'.

In all their songs, as in their dances, the negroes never lost the wonderful sense of rhythm they had inherited from their ancestors in Africa. Their varied time-patterns owed much of their excitement to syncopation, a rhythmical device for avoiding flat-footed obviousness by finding unexpected accents between the main beats of the bar. This was the foundation of jazz.

Jazz is now a commercial industry: the excitement of improvisation is too often lost in the process of 'canning'; and in much recorded jazz the rhythm has become routine. But when jazz is performed by an artist in his own right surroundings the true rhythmic vitality remains.

Jazz has influenced many composers both in America and in Europe for more than fifty years and has helped, in its own way, to bring about the new music of the twentieth century.

The melancholy of jazz – symbolised by the French artist Matisse
from Matisse: 'Jazz'. Copyright S.P.A.D.E.M., Paris

The syncopation of modern jazz owes much to the swinging rhythms and energetic time-patterns of ancient African dances and drum-beats.

Composer; Performer; Listener

When a composer sets out to write a piece of music he is usually quite definite about what he is going to create; for although music is intangible there is nothing vague about it. A composer has to be a practical workman. He may, for instance, be asked to write an opera for a particular occasion. For this he would need the help of many other practical artists. Here is the kind of way in which an opera could be made, from its very first idea to its actual presentation on the stage of an opera-house.

The composer will probably begin by drawing up a time-schedule of work, as if he were an architect-builder. Then he finds the right librettist to work with, and they discuss the chosen story in detail, plan its general outline, and divide it into scenes – even into arias, recitatives and choruses. When the

librettist has written his first draft of the words the composer studies it, pointing out weak syllables that destroy the rhythm, or clusters of consonants that would be unsingable. As soon as the libretto is satisfactory the composer begins to set it to music, working at it day after day until it is finished.

He writes his first sketches in 'short score', roughly indicating the instruments that are to play, but keeping the notes to two or three staves. When he gets to the end of each of the acts he plays it through on the piano to the producer and the principal singers in the cast.

The music is copied out and duplicated and the singers learn their parts. Meanwhile the scenery and costumes will have been designed: the designer will have had to work in close consultation with the

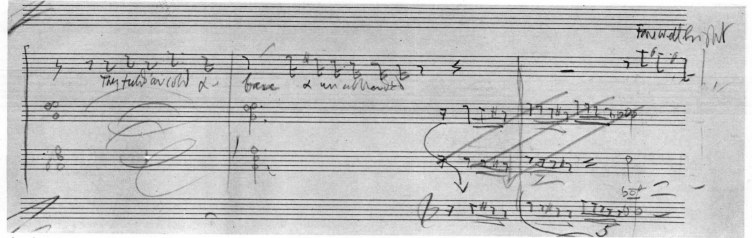

Any line in the rough sketch of a modern opera may be altered several times before it satisfies both its composer and his fellow artists.

producer, to avoid making mistakes – such as putting a solid piece of scenery where it prevents the heroine watching the conductor's beat.

The composer will by then have written the full score – a task that may take weeks or months of continual work, all day, every day and half the night. He will then go through the score with the conductor: the parts will be copied: the orchestra will rehearse in the pit of the empty opera-house; and when the moment comes for the curtain to go up on the opening night, the combined efforts of all those taking part will bring the composer's ideas to life.

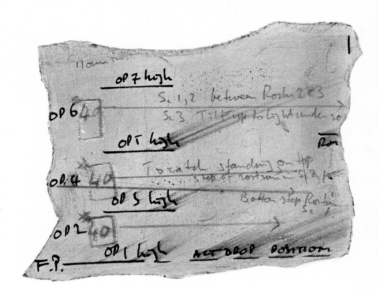

Ceri Richards
Artist-craftsmen have to plan operatic stage-designs and lighting-plots (like those on this page) in close consultation with the composer.

64

Every composer is utterly dependent on the performers who bring his music to life. Galerie Louis Carré, Paris (Louis Laniepce)

Lotte Meitner-Graf
The greatest violinists in the world practise technique day after day.

A painter hangs his finished picture on a wall, and everyone can see it. A composer writes a work, but no one can hear it until it is performed. Professional singers and players have great responsibilities; for the composer is utterly dependent on them. A student of music needs as long and as arduous a training to become a performer as a medical student needs to become a doctor.

Most training is concerned with technique, for musicians have to have the muscular proficiency of an athlete or a ballet dancer. Singers practise breathing every day, as their vocal chords would be inadequate without the controlled muscular support of their diaphragm. Learners of brass instruments have to practise controlling their lip-muscles. Oboists have to get used to holding their breath in reserve until they reach the end of a phrase – a process that has been compared with having to learn to swim under water.

Violinists and other string players practise moving the fingers of the left hand up and down, while drawing the bow to and fro with the right arm: these two entirely different movements have to be controlled as if they were one – rather like performing a conjuring trick while walking a tight-rope.

All instrumentalists have to practise technique every day. If you could stand outside the door while one of the greatest violinists in the world was practising, you would almost certainly hear him playing two or three notes of a scale or of an arpeggio, *very* slowly, over and over again.

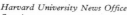

Great artists can thoroughly enjoy performing music of any age.
Lotte Meitner-Graf

Singers and instrumentalists have to be able to get every note perfectly in tune. Pianists are spared this particular anxiety, for the notes are already there, waiting for them; and it is the piano-tuner's responsibility to tune their instrument for them. But they have their own difficulties. In a smooth, flowing melody the hammers that hit the strings have to be coaxed not to sound like percussion. And pianists have to unravel the overlapping lines of counterpoint, so that each 'voice' keeps its individuality.

This problem of getting clear texture is one of the many that confront the student-conductor: he has to learn to know every note of the music and how it should sound, and he has to aim at controlling these

sounds with fanatical but utterly selfless authority.

Technique is no use unless it is combined with musical knowledge and understanding. Great artists are those who are so thoroughly at home in the language of music that they can enjoy performing works written in any century.

During the last sixty or seventy years there has been a good deal of interest in the revival of early music. Many performers spend all the free time they can spare in exploring manuscripts and volumes of music in the famous libraries of the world; where unknown masterpieces may be waiting for the skill and patience and enthusiasm that perhaps, one day, will bring them back to life.

Harvard University News Office
Students at a seminar in the music library at Harvard, where a special study is made of editing early music for present-day performance.

More people go to concerts in the 20th century than ever before.
Courtesy Life Magazine (Walter Sanders)

Record sleeve: copyright Club Français du Disque, Paris

B Johann Sebastian Bach / Prélude et Fugue
en mi mineur / Partita en fa mineur
Sonate en trio n° 5 en do majeur / Trois chorals

The revival of old music has had one great draw-back: it has set up a false distinction between 'music' and 'contemporary music'. Over a century ago there was no such barrier and 'music' meant the music that was being written at the time. But in our own century most concert-goers think of contemporary music as something unusual – outside the normal repertoire. The majority of the vast new audiences of radio and gramophone listeners agrees with them, preferring programmes that keep to familiar composers such as Beethoven and Tchaikovsky.

Twentieth-century music has therefore started at a disadvantage. And, unfortunately, it has made matters worse for itself by often sounding so strange. Some of the early twentieth-century experiments in distortion were such shocks when they were first performed that, as with cubism in painting, it has taken years for the works to be appreciated.

Experiments have been made in three keys, in no keys, in quarter-tones, in borrowings from ragtime and borrowings from blues, in back-to-Bach and back-to-Gregorian-plainchant, in machine-music – made out of gun-fire, factory sirens and ship's whistles – and in electronic music, which is so far the only experiment that is a direct result of the mechanical reproduction of music.

Some twentieth-century experiments have been short-lived; others, such as writing in many keys, have been absorbed into the music of today where they have become so familiar that they no longer cause any discomfort to listeners.

One entirely new method of writing music has developed during the last half-century. This is the

Vast modern audiences listen to records and radio broadcasts, yet not many people are familiar with the music of living composers.
R. L. Jarmain

twelve-note or twelve-tone system which has broken right away from the traditions of two thousand years. The system is not founded on the seven-note scale with UT as its focal point; it is founded on the division of the octave into twelve notes a semitone apart, each note being equally important. The notes are not used as degrees of a chromatic scale; they are arranged in a fixed order such as:

Eb G A B C♯ C♮ Bb D E♮ F♯ G♯ F♮

Any similar row or series of twelve notes can be used forwards, backwards and upside-down as the material out of which 'serial' music is constructed.

It is impossible for anyone to say whether this is to be the recognised music of the second half of the twentieth century. Some musicians think it is. Some think that there are still unlimited possibilities in the seven-note scale and the chords that grow out of it. Some think that it does not matter what style a composer chooses to write in, as long as he has something definite to say and says it clearly.

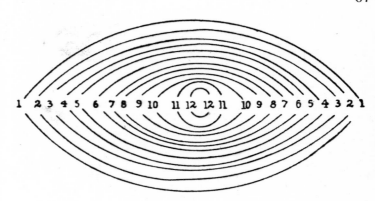

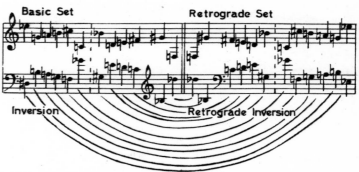

An example of a twelve-tone row from music by Arnold Schoenberg
Courtesy Ernest Benn, Ltd., Schoenberg: 'Style and Idea'

Picasso painting: Museum of Modern Art, New York. Mrs. Simon Guggenheim Fund
Distortion in new music, like that in cubist painting, was at first so startling that it took time for people to appreciate its strange beauty.

Although no one can tell what the future of music may be, there can be no doubt that the present day is an exciting time for composers and performers and audiences. The language of music is becoming more and more widely known. School orchestras are now taken just as much for granted as school classes in drawing and painting. Music-making in the home is as flourishing as ever, in spite of what people say about this being an age of passive entertainment. Composers are writing for combined amateur orchestras and choirs, with choruses in which the audience is invited to join in the singing.

Although music is flourishing, many people worry about the question of state support for the arts – whether it should or should not be given and where the money is to come from. Without some such support, many opera companies and orchestras would find it impossible to survive: the great private patrons no longer exist.

Conditions of work are changing for musicians, and it seems that we may be experiencing the beginnings of an entirely new form of musical patronage. It has been said that 'the interesting stage has now been reached when the artist, whether composer or performer, is himself undertaking a certain amount of patronage, providing opportunities for musicians to become for once in a while amateurs – that is, lovers of music – and to play or sing or compose for the glory of their art and without thought of the morrow'.

If this is true, and we think it is, we shall soon find ourselves living in another golden age of music.

Terence Le Goubin
Combined school orchestras at a music festival. Scenes like this confirm the belief that music-making is flourishing today as much as ever.

K. Hutton

INDEX

Page-numbers refer to the most detailed description of each item.

On page 24 the French song is from an example quoted by J. A. Westrup from a manuscript in the Bibliothèque Nationale, Paris (New Oxford History of Music, Volume II); the German song is from Denkmäler der Tonkunst in Oesterreich, Volume 37, (i).